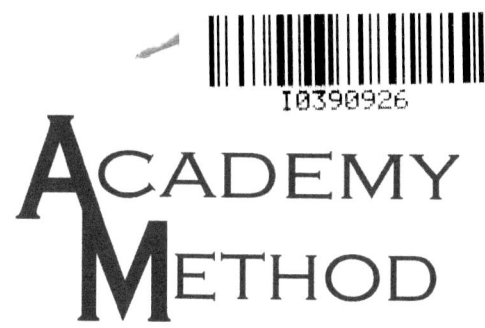

ACADEMY METHOD

BARRE EXERCISES
AND
STRUCTURE

By
Ken Ludden

A FONTEYN ACADEMY PRESS PUBLICATION

This book is intended as a textbook companion to the Academy
Method Instructor Certification Program and should not be used for
any other purpose.

First published by Lulu, February 16, 2013
ISBN: 978-1-300-73173-3

Printed in the United States of America

A FONTEYN ACADEMY PRESS PUBLICATION

Table of Contents

HOW TO USE THIS BOOK

Originally intended for teacher training, this text can be very useful to students. There is some technical information presented that will not be the direct concern of the student of classical theatrical dancing, but much of the information presented is very useful.

When you know what you are doing, why you are doing it, how to do it, and what it is used for, then everything you do has direct purpose. You can focus your intent and be aware precisely when you have achieved a goal. It is in this spirit that we have published this book and made it available to students of classical theatrical dance.

Students of The Margot Fonteyn Academy of Ballet will find it useful when preparing for exams as well, for it gives correct spellings of French terms (mandatory for MFAB students), and the academic information on which they are tested throughout the school session and in final exams.

If you fit into neither of these categories, and are just a lover of ballet, then you will find this information of some little fascination when you go to the theater to watch a performance. You will understand some of the technical fine points of classical dance, and see how they have, or have not, been incorporated into the work of different artists.

Structuring Barre Exercises and Sequences

One of the unique elements of the Academy Method is that classes are structured. As such, each class has a specific goal and focus, based on the developmental process of the dancers in the class, the demands on them or in relation to particular choreography they must dance.

In this book you will begin to learn the purpose of specific *barre* exercises, and other elements that might be considered when structuring a class around a movement element or theme.

Barre Purpose

Each exercise at the *barre* has a direct application to danced steps in the center, and no matter what exact combination is given, each exercise will always fulfill a direct application in its nature.

Thematic Structure

Yet beneath that broad canopy, it is possible to create combinations at the *barre* that are custom designed for particular needs. As you study the different exercises, their purpose and what is involved in their proper execution, imagine a few different scenarios that might occur in the life of a dance student, and imagine what you would do to accommodate those.

Some examples might be a class in winter and the heater isn't working too well, or any one of the following: final exam week, preparing to dance at an outdoor festival on the grass, or it is the last class before summer vacation and the kids are all excited about a dance intensive they will be taking out of town. What would you give in class? How would you structure the class in each of these situations?

Consider, too, the different struggles dancers have, such as: improper placement, popping rib cage, droopy arms, unpointed toes in jumps, inability to stay balanced, falling out of turns, etc. Each of these is due to a wrongly applied force, improper alignment, lack of force to one part of the body, favoring one side, etc. Once you determine the weakness, bad habit, wrongly applied force, lack of force, or skewed impetus for a turn then imagine what sort of class you would give, thematically, to address such issues.

But first, let's look at the basic exercises in the *barre* work, and the other elements that go into the process of deciding how to select a theme, and then how to structure the class around that theme.

EXERCISES AT THE BARRE

Every exercise at the *barre* has a direct application to the steps done in the center, or the infinite variety of movements invented by choreographers. Your dance students must understand these relationships, and learn to make use of them. Give them quizzes and tests of these. Should they one day audition to attend the Academy, they will be required to know these things very well.

PURPOSE OF EACH EXERCISE

Students who know what the exercises are for, and how they are intended to be used, will be at a great advantage when a new step isn't going well. They will be able to figure out how to correct a step, or be more likely to be able to, they will know what to ask of an outside viewer of their attempt and they will understand the corrections you and other teachers give them. Once corrected, they will know how to prepare for class, which muscles or actions to give outside attention to, and what to work on more at the *barre*. Then getting into class will become an effort with great purpose and specific personal goals. It gives them the keys to being a very good dancer.

Below is the list of exercises at the *barre* and their direct relationship to dance movement.

GRAND PLIÉ

Grand: big; *Plié*: bend

PURPOSE—1) TO STRETCH THE ACHILLES TENDON; 2) TO ESTABLISH CONTROL OVER BODY

Grand plié is for stretching the Achilles tendon, and the dancer establishing control over the body and its movements.

In the Academy Method, *grand plié* is done without *porte de bras* other than simply breathing the arm over the legs. The knees must be aligned over the toes and the heels must either press down into the floor, or, when lifted in the course of the movement, they must reach for it. The pace of the movement is steady, slow and consistent. It does not stop at the bottom, nor at the top, and each extremity of movement is reached just in time to reverse the movement and continue.

The movement from the base of the *plié* and starting back up is the part that will give your dancers the power in their jumps. They must not bounce out of the bottom, rush to straight legs, or sit at the top.

Any time they look down at their feet their hips, shoulders or some other part of their body will go backward to counterbalance that weight change. Likewise, the knees must always travel in the same direction as the toes are pointing. Always!

They must keep the knee caps engaged at all times, and for those with hyper-extended legs, they must never allow the legs to collapse backward at the knees.

NOTE: It cannot be over-emphasized the importance of consistency of movement here. The body travels at one, constant speed to the bottom of the *plié* and back up. Movement does not stop at the top or the bottom, other than the natural moment of stillness when the apex and nadir are reached and the direction of the continuous movement is reversed. Students, also, must not disengage from their bodies at either top or bottom of the *plié*. In fact, maintaining control and active connection with the pelvis and legs at the base of the *plié*, and the maintenance of consistent speed when starting back upward again builds the strength for all landings in jumps and the power for propulsion into the air.

DEMI PLIÉ

Demi: half; *Plié*: bend

PURPOSE: 1) LANDING FROM JUMPS, 2) JUMPING INTO THE AIR

Demi plié is for landing from jumps and jumping into the air. The movement is accomplished by first lifting the stomach and relaxing the legs so the knees can bend with ease. Knee caps are always engaged here too.

Each *demi plié* has four parts:

1) with torso actively lifted up, relax the knees and drop directly to the bottom of the *plié*;

2) press the heels into the floor while deepening the bend of the knees;

3) straighten the knees by pushing down on the floor with the heels while lifting the knee caps and top of the head quickly (but softly) to straight legs; and

4) lift the body taller by pulling in the stomach muscles and stretching the spine long through the top of the head.

Be very sure to remind the students to keep their heels pressed firmly into the floor beneath them. Concentrate on the bottom of the *plié*, both getting there quickly, and pressing the heels more. Say the words in every class many times, and find a dancer to correct specifically about this in nearly every class. Give the correction from across the room so that all can hear, and change which dancer you remind so that nobody feels picked on.

Particularly in third and fifth positions, check the back heel, because this is the one that is often forgotten. Make sure the body weight is centered on both feet evenly, and that it is distributed evenly across the entire soles of both feet. But also check that the back heel is firmly pressed into the ground. It is easy to look only at the ankles and feet here and miss the fact that the dancer has shifted their pelvis over the back foot. When giving this correction and watching progress, then, stand back from the dancer so that in your periphery you will see their entire body. Also have them demonstrate it starting with straight legs, so that if there is a shifting backward of the weight you will catch it.

Use of very clear music is essential for this exercise. Choose music for your pianist (or on an album) that has the internal rhythm evident, so that the moment to press the heels into the ground while deepening the *plié* is obvious. You must immediately notice, in combinations in the center, anyone who is lacking a bottom from which to find the impetus for lift in the strong bottom of the *plié*. Be on the lookout for this. Allow nothing to escape your notice, and bring everything you see back to the *barre* in the next class. Dancers cannot dance without a solid *demi plié*.

NOTE: In both *grand plié* and *demi plié* there is a sensation of lifting so high at the top that the knees must bend. This develops as the body learns the movements, and the proper muscles become strong. At the top of the *plié* the dancer must actively lift higher through the spine and top of the head before the descent begins anew. The dancer has indeed lifted up so much that the legs are free below and the knees just fall open, for the combination of strong erector spine muscles and psoas together can actually lift the pelvis up off of the femur bones in the hips. This is discovered slowly by dancers, and you must continually use phrases like "lift so tall your legs fall open" and "lift over the top", etc.

BATTEMENT CLOCHE

Battement: hit, strike, swing; *Cloche:* bell

PURPOSE: 1) FREE THE HIP; 2) MOVE LEG AS SINGLE UNIT

Battement cloche prepares the body for freedom in the hip, and to move the legs as a unit in a way that does not disrupt balance, placement or momentum in other parts of the body.

Cloche is the French word for "bell" and in this movement the leg and foot represent the clapper in the dome of the bell.

It must be done from the tip of the toe, and as the leg passes through the first position you will be able to see who is lifting a hip, collapsing into the lower back or hyper-extending their legs.

NOTE: *Battement Cloche* is listed here in the sequence of *barre* structure, and with dancers who are trained in the Western style of classical dance you may need this to get the hips moving feely. Indeed, with students trained from the start in the Academy Method, the *grand battement* is to be the third exercise at the *barre*, except when circumstances demand otherwise, or the theme of the class is best realized with an early lift of the hips prior to that accomplished with *grand battement*.

GRAND BATTEMENT

Grand: big; *Battement:* hit, strike, swing

PURPOSE: LIFT PELVIS UPWARD

Grand battement is defined as: the largest movement of the leg possible that does not upset balance, or cause another part of the body to become disturbed. It is done on the upbeat of the music.

The purpose of *grand battement* is to lift the pelvis. The movement is initiated by a quick strike of the big toe downward into the ground while relaxing the muscles of the hip. Like a *frappé* that is only done with the foot. This sudden and sharp movement is the impetus for the full *grand battement*.

The leg goes from static on the ground, with the heel firmly planted, to the very top of the movement instantaneously, and then the leg is controlled as it floats down, arriving in time to become static, with the heel again firmly on the ground.

Grand battement on the <u>upbeat</u> of the music is the same exact movement used for large jumps. And as the body must be the music, the movement into the air must be very fast so that the body and music are one.

When teaching *grand battement* watch the spot in the air where the foot will be at the top of the movement. If you do not see the foot on the upbeat, then the exercise has been a waste of time for the dancer. Hold them to the test of being the music, and the leg arriving where it should, when it should.

But don't be fooled. Once you have seen to it that the legs are arriving at the top of the movement at the right time, then look at the feet on the floor. Be sure that they are waiting until the precise moment of the upbeat to do the movement. If they have gotten the leg up on the upbeat by starting early, and then all they have done is shift the over-muscled movement in the music so it will look right, but they are still doing a sluggish, ineffective movement.

Grand battement must be done from the very tips of the toes, and each one must come from a stillness in which the weight of the leg is firmly on the ground. Instruct the students to keep the leg close, and fully stretched. They should attempt to get taller as they do each one.

Also, dancers must imagine that each *grand battement* goes underground on the way up, which will enforce the use of a *frappé* with the ankle only to serve as impetus for each movement. Likewise, when the leg comes down, by imagining that it goes beneath the surface of the floor, it will cause them to end with the heel planted firmly down.

> NOTE: The foot of the working leg must be still at the bottom of the movement at the same time as the leg is at its full height. This appears to be a physical impossibility, but in a fully trained dancer, the time it takes to get the leg from planted on the ground to the peek of the movement is less than 1/100th of a second. This is only possible if the upward swing is caused by the simultaneous firing of the *sartorius* and *flexor digitora*.

TWO-COUNT GRAND BATTEMENT

PURPOSE: 1) LIFT PELVIS INTO AIR; 2) EMBELLISH THE CREST OF ARC

A two-count *grand battement* is a legitimate movement, but should be done more in the center floor than at the *barre*. Sometimes, depending on the theme of the class and the developmental needs of the dancers, it may be worked into a normal *grand battement* combination at the *barre*. Often, by placing two similar but different movements together forces the dancer to distinguish all of the nuanced differences between them.

Still used in dancing for lifting the hips into the air, the two-count *grand battement* lifts quickly to the very top of the movement <u>on the beat</u> (as opposed to the upbeat), then stops at the top of the movement and holds still in the air, then is let to drop down to the closed position. The two-count *grand battement* is used when dancers are getting to the top of their jumps in the center, but are not able to achieve either the "hang time" at the crest, or are not crafting a well-shaped trajectory arc with the movement. You may also need to do these in class when dancers are not getting proper *batterie* in their big jumps, do not have time for double air turns or other actions that embellish the crest of jumps.

> NOTE: Never give fewer than 8 *grand battement en croix* in a class, and it is best to give 16 *en croix*, on both sides. *Grand battement* done incorrectly will harm the dancers. When you give 8 or more *grand battement* on the upbeat, it is impossible for dancers to do them incorrectly throughout. The more of these the dancer does in a combination, and the more tired the muscles become, the greater efficiency the body will find in doing the movement and soon they will soon be executed correctly.

TENDU

Tendu: stretch

PURPOSE: ASSURE FOOT IS POINTED WHEN LEAVING GROUND IN JUMPS

Tendu means "to stretch" and it refers to stretching the full leg, including the foot to the toe, in as long and straight a line possible. The purpose for a *tendu* is to make sure that when the foot leaves the ground in a jump that it is fully pointed.

The *tendu* is accomplished when the toe presses down into the floor to create impetus for movement in a *frappé* like movement, while being sure that the foot points as a single unit. As it is for jumping, it is important that the rhythm in the body is that of a jump and that the moment the heel touches the ground the toe activates.

It is very good to intermix heel drops with rebounded *tendues* so that the dancers develop a sense of the heel dropping down and bouncing. Also, *tendu* teaches that it is the activation of the foot strike along with the lift in the standing hip that creates soft quickness and stability.

> NOTE: The movement of a *tendu* is a down-up movement of the heel, NOT an in-out movement of the leg. And the only action in a *tendu* is the crisp percussive pointing of the full foot causing the movement of the leg to happen. The action of closing the leg is achieved by completely relaxing the hip, rather than using the ham strings to slam the heel down.

REBOUNDED TENDU

PURPOSE: TO ACTIVATE POINT OF FOOT IMMEDIATELY UPON LANDING IN CONSECUTIVE JUMPS

In a rebounded *tendu* the exercises begins in a full *battement tendu* position, and from there the heel bounces off of the floor. The bounce is on the beat, and the full bounce of the *tendu* happens on that same beat, as with the *grand battement*. The foot must simultaneously be in the closed position with the heel on the ground and the fully stretched position. If done correctly this action does not include any of the primary muscles and so can be done in a fraction of a second, feeling as though it is simultaneous.

Be certain that the dancers have the proper shape of the foot, and that the Achilles tendon isn't engaged, thereby exposing the fact that the foot is being improperly pointed. You must also check that the hips are level and undisturbed by the movement.

The movement is very soft and blindingly fast. The entire foot must work as a whole, not broken into parts.[1]

---

[1] The action of breaking the *tendu* into segments and involving the ball of the foot is part of training for *pointe* work, and then is done with a specific rhythm.

TWO-COUNT TENDU

PURPOSE: TO MAKE SURE THE POINTING OF THE FOOT COMES FROM A HEEL SOLIDLY ON THE GROUND

The two-count *tendu* begins from a closed position (though that is not a rule, as there are some times the combination works better to begin in an open position) with the heel firmly on the ground. The percussive strike of the toe pressing into the floor causing the leg to move into a *battement tendu* position takes the leg to a position where the toe is firmly pressed into the floor to create the movement, but at the crest of the arc the toe is touching the floor but without pressure. Stretch the leg long in that position.

Then lift tall on the standing leg and completely relax the working leg so that the heel drops to the floor instantaneously.[2] Then press the heel firmly into the ground so that the next percussive strike of the foot comes from a leg with the heel firmly pressed into the ground.

This exercise has an anatomy quite like *demi-plié*.

1) push down with the toe to cause the leg to move;

2) stretch the leg long all the way to the tip of the toe;

3) drop the heel back to the closed position by lifting and releasing the working hip; and

4) press the heel into the floor.

NOTE: Be sure that the body position is 1ˢᵗ throughout, even if you start in 3ʳᵈ or 5ᵗʰ position, the standing leg must lift to full 1ˢᵗ position during the exercise.

---

[2] Remember that mass falls to gravity at the rate of 32′ per second, per second. Any muscle involvement will slow the closing of the leg and take away the soft naturalness of the movement.

DEMI-PLIÉ TENDU

PURPOSE: TO CREATE CORRECT BEGINNING FOR *JETÉ SAUTÉ* AND *ASSEMBLÉ*

In *demi plié—tendu* exercises be sure that the internal anatomy of the *demi plié* is fully adhered to. The legs must both straighten at the exact same time and at the exact same speed in a fully coordinated movement. Be sure the hips do not travel either toward the working leg or away from it, for some dancers have been taught to "work the floor" in this exercise and consequently begin with a *chassée*, causing displacement of the hips.

The primary objective in this exercise is to establish a relationship between the two forces of lift needed for steps such as: *jeté sauté, assemblé sauté, brissé, sauté ronde de jambe en l'air, sissone ouverte, cabriole, gagliarde, sissone battue,* and other such jumps. In each of these the dancer must use the combination of two sources of lift to properly execute the movement—lift of propulsion, or thrust, from downward *frappé*, and the pelvic lift from a *grand battement* action when the *dégagé* movement is freed to become a greater lift but is then suddenly arrested at *battement glissé* height. The combination of lift and propulsion, or thrust, in these steps begins with *demi-plié tendu*.

DÉGAGÉ

Dégagé: to disengage (toe from floor)

PURPOSE: TO UN-POINT THE FOOT QUICKLY WHEN LANDING FROM JUMPS

Dégagé is done by the very fast and percussive downward strike of the toe against the floor that causes the leg to move outward, but only so far that the toe is a paper-width from the floor. This is the same distance from the floor in *Petit Allegro* steps in classical dance. To accomplish this, the hip must be completely relaxed and the upper body must be lifted.

The *dégagé* is accented inward and downward, like the landing of very quick *changements*. It is very important that *dégagé* is given at a very quick tempo at the *barre*, even if at first the younger dancers cannot manage it without wiggling their hips. Give this exercise either with the arm in *bras bas* or in the lateral lift arm position.[3] And if you give any *porte de bras* with *dégagé*, have it be 2nd *porte de bras* with consecutive *dégagé à la seconde*.

Repetition is paramount with *dégagé* in particular because if the foot cannot un-point quickly that means that the foot is improperly pointed using the *gastrocnemius* muscles causing the Achilles tendon to be engaged each time. When landing from jumps with an engaged Achilles tendon, the tendon is pulled on each and every time and eventually it begins to degrade.

Dégagé is given with Bug Squashers, quick and small *battement cloche*, *pas de cheval,* and other quick movements. But these combinations come after the students can execute very fast *dégagé* without it affecting their hips at all, having the foot fully and properly pointed each time, with the heel firmly down on every closing.

---

[3] Lateral Arm Lift Position – approached out of 1st *porte de bras*, this position is when the shoulder to elbow line is parallel to the floor and going directly to the side of the body, and the arm is bent back in on itself so that the fingertips rest lightly on the shoulder.

RONDE DE JAMBE

Ronde: around; De: of; Jambe: leg

PURPOSE: TURNING MOTION AND IMPETUS

It is imperative that all *ronde de jambe* exercises are done from 1st position. The working leg must pass directly from front to back in alignment with the working hip, and at no time does it cross to the front of the body, nor does the hip move.

All preparations for *ronde de jambe* in the Academy Method are done from 1st position as well. And they are normally done to a slow or moderate waltz (though this is a rule sometimes broken with the students are very young and just learning how to manage the exercise).

Each beat of the waltz measure has a corresponding position which the leg passes through at that moment. However, the movement is one speed with no accents, accelerations or stops. It is a smooth, regular, even, and consistent rotation of the leg through fixed points at precise counts in the music. No exercise is as clear, and no exercise is as abused by student and professional attempts to perform it.

Ronde de jambe can be done either direction—*en dedans, or en dehors*—and is often done with the arm *à la seconde*

To begin the *ronde de jambe en dehors*, the working leg is behind in *pointe tendu quatrième en arrière*. On <u>COUNT ONE</u> it passes through first position and arrives at *quatrième devant à terre,* the movement through 1st position carried to the front by pressure down into the floor with the big toe of the working leg. The leg does not stop here, though it arrives on the count fully *pointe*d, instead the upper chest lifts up and forward giving the leg impetus to move outside around to *à la seconde* where it arrives on COUNT TWO. Again it does not stop but continues on to arrive at *pointe tendu quatrième en arrière* at COUNT THREE.

This completes one *ronde de jambe à terre*. Consistent with the exercise thus far, it does not stop but passes through 1st position to repeat the circuit.

The *ronde de jambe en dedans à terre* is the exact reverse of that *en dehors* with one very significant exception. The impetus for the *ronde de jambe en dedans à terre* is the pulling close of the leg while rotating the heel forward to start the circuit around.

Watch carefully for the following common errors, which must be caught early or they become bad habits that seriously hinder the dancer's ability to: perform turns, establish proper balance and placement, and many other things.

FIRST, be sure that the dancers do not move their hips;

SECOND, watch that the feet are fully pointed before the leg starts its circular movement either direction (though the full pointing of the foot done as the circular movement begins gives it an accent that is quirky but has an appeal);

THIRD, be sure the leg remains straight at all times, particularly in the back;

FORTH, make very certain that the trajectory of movement from front to back (or back to front) is a straight line without any movement at the extremities toward the center of the body, and that the leg is aligned with the center of the working hip;

FIFTH, be certain that the dancer is standing in a full 1st position posture throughout; and

SIXTH, make sure that the movement is smooth, controlled, perpetual and without any sense of accent.

The impetus for each direction of the *ronde de jambe* is radically different and must be carefully learned.

For *ronde de jambe en dehors* (opening from the front of the body and traveling around to the back), the forward movement of the upper chest, or sternum, is the impetus. It is imperative that the movement of the chest is up and forward, rather than simply forward or forward and down. Be careful that the dancers do not tilt their pelvis forward with this movement, or rock back on their standing leg.

For *ronde de jambe en dedans* (closing the leg from the back around to the front), the impetus is in the forward rotation of the heel, keeping the knee fully stretched and the leg pulled in to the hip socket. Be certain that the hips do not twist to do this. It is easy for the heel to take the lead from just behind the *à la seconde* position on the way around, but this is too late and means that the *quadriceps* and hip have been the impetus for the movement.

> NOTE: This is a very difficult exercise for new students to achieve, primarily because it is the most complex of the training exercises for the body. Be patient.

RONDE DE JAMBE EN L'AIR
Ronde: around; *De*: of; *Jambe*: leg; *En*: in; *l'air*: the air

PURPOSE: TO CREATE CIRCULAR MOMENTUM THAT CAN BE EASILY TRANSFERRED

Ronde de jambe en l'air is a fast, smooth circular movement of the lower leg that is done when the leg itself is being held *à la seconde*. Each revolution of the lower leg brings the toe of the working leg to brush (literally) the belly of the calf of the standing leg. This movement establishes the level of the leg, which is not hip height, yet higher than *glissé* level. In consecutive repetitions of this movement, the final one may be released into a *grand battement*.

Throughout this exercise, the line of the working leg from hip to knee is maintained without any movement; the leg does not lift, it does not drop and it does not turn-in or turn-out. The actual trajectory of the toe is in a circular movement that is 10" (ten inches) in diameter, with the inner most part where the toe brushes the belly of the calf of the standing leg. The back of this circular movement is placed from the position of the foot when it is brought from the *à la seconde* placement in, never crossing behind the shadow of the upper leg, and the remainder of the circular movement is in front of the leg.

The movement itself is caused by gravity. When the lower leg is released, it will fall directly to the point where the toe brushes the belly of the calf. There is a natural rebound to this gravity-spurred movement, and the dancer must direct the momentum of that rebound into the appropriate circular path, and then just apply the slightest energy of the *sartorius* to fully stretch the leg.

The tear-drop shape of the movement helps propel it as well. And the overall rhythm of the movement is a relaxed whosh-lift [hold], whosh-lift [hold], etc.

In the double *ronde de jambe en l'air*, the circular movement is continued with so little actual muscular involvement that it feels as though merely intending that the movement will repeat is enough impetus for it to do so. It is a very light, easy and natural movement.

GRAND RONDE DE JAMBE

Grand: big; *Ronde*: around; *De*: of; *Jambe*: leg

PURPOSE: TO COUNTERBALANCE THE FULLEST CIRCULAR MOVEMENT OF THE LEG WITH THE TORSO

Grand Ronde de Jambe is a study of counterbalance, and is a smooth, uninterrupted journey of the inevitability of line and expression. Solidly atop the standing leg, the fully extended working leg is counterbalanced by the torso as the leg works its way from front to back (*en dehors*) or back to front (*en dedans*).

The most remarkable specific is that the body balances toward the working leg throughout. The impetus for the movement *en dehors* is the lift up and forward of the upper chest; and the impetus for the movement *en dedans* is the heel being brought forward.

This movement is most often done as an adagio movement, or in partnering. But it is also done as an ending of a *pirouette* in which the centrifugal force is transferred outward to the leg and the counterbalance of torso to leg movement holds the body in stasis with a blissful sense of balance.

ADAGIO

Adagio: slowly

PURPOSE: TO PREPARE FOR *PETIT ALLEGRO* MOVEMENTS

Adagio is a type of movement rather than a specific exercise. In these exercises, movements and their mechanics are slowed down greatly and care is given that each part of the body is in perfect synch with the whole. The overall coordination of the arms, legs, torso, hips, attitude and trajectory are made visible and laid naked by the slow tempo.

Here it is possible for you, as a teacher, to see exactly where things are going wrong for a student, and how they might be corrected. When preparing your class, know the objectives you need to address, and the specific problems your different students have. Design exercises that strengthen weaknesses, but also that demand the precise action of the students they are having trouble with.

Do not be afraid to ask them to move slowly, hold positions a long time, or work to an extreme of balance. If there is a quicker movement or type of movement that is consistently problematic, design an *Adagio* that will uncover the problem, or strengthen the weak link.

Adagios are about mechanics and phrasing.

FRAPPÉ

Frappé: to slap, hit, strike

PURPOSE: PUSHING DIRECTLY DOWNWARD TO CAUSE PROPULSION OR THRUST, AND LIFT

The *frappé* is an exact replica of what one leg does in a simple *sauté*. The leg bends at hip, knee and ankle, and then simultaneously all work together to push directly downward with great speed. This is then applied to dancing to cause propulsion, thrust, and/or lift. The movement caused depends on the exact angle downward the particular *frappé* achieves..

When done one leg at a time, the direction of the leg must travel away from down, or the dancer will break their toe running it into the ground. This new direction achieves a quite familiar position, being exactly the same as that in a *dégagé*. The toe must travel off of the floor no more than the width of a single piece of paper. If a dancer is to jump and go up into the air, then they must push directly down. In fact, whatever the direction of the push, the body will travel in the opposite direction.

The *frappé* anatomy is more about rhythm than mechanics or shape. When dancers jump into the air they must keep their legs straight and their toes pointed. Hence, the entire strike is done on the COUNT OF &- and then the leg is sharply out, with the toe a paper width from the floor, for COUNTS ONE THROUGH FOUR and then the next flex strike occurs again on COUNT & leading to the following COUNT ONE.

The inward position of the working leg, before the strike, is fully flexed. In this position, the 5th metatarsal bone rests on the top of the arch of the standing foot.

> NOTE: Be certain that, when seen from the front, the heel is fully visible having crossed past the calf of the standing leg each time.

ALLEGRETTO

Allegretto: little, fast

PURPOSE: CENTER THE BODY, USE THE BODY WORK AS A SINGLE ORGANISM

The *barre* ends with small, fast movements. These are movements that make the whole body move as a whole, and force the dancer to let go of the *barre*. The dancers are about to move to the center floor, and they cannot take the *barre* with them. And so to give them small fast jumps and turns bridges the gap well.

It also accomplishes getting them to be oriented standing on their own feet, finding their own center of balance and shifting from movements that are basically stationary to those that will move in space across the floor.

All *allegretto* steps involve jumping, turning or *relevé*. In all of these the dancer must lead with the top of the head, and execute the movement so that the knee caps arrive first. They also involve actions, placement or arrested actions of the arms as part of the movement. Previous steps at the *barre* have required use of the *barre* to do them in such a way that the muscles are developed. Now, by the end of *barre*, they need to feel both arms working in unison with the entire body. Also at this point the muscles that have been worked on individually at the *barre* must now join the whole body in whatever state they have achieved. The dancer must become oriented to how these newly worked muscles move and feel before they enter the center floor.

STRETCH

Between *barre* and center, having worked each muscle and muscle group separately, it is time to stretch the fully oxygenated muscles to prepare for dancing. In the section on stretch there are many exercises to work from.

Repetition and Memory

Dancers must develop "muscle memory" in order to meet the demands of a career. The moment a dancer's career begins, s/he is required to learn new choreography quickly, and often dancers are left to their own devices to perfect the new material learned. This is a difficult task, and many careers are short lived due to failure in this department. The body is very complex and it is impossible for a person to think of every muscle involved in a movement, as well as all of the other information needed to dance a role in a ballet.

The development of muscle memory begins at the very start of one's period of study as a student. As we will see later, all ballet steps are broken down into the various functions different individual muscles and body parts must perform. The classical form demands that each muscle, joint, tendon and ligament works to the maximum degree without altering neighboring parts of the body. Therefore, each muscle must learn to work automatically, and to its maximum.

Repetition

For any movement to become automatic, meaning that the person doing the movement does not consciously think about the its execution, it must be repeated 100,000 times. In training a dancer, this is done through repetition.

For example, a *tendu* is included in most steps in dancing. If a dancer is given two combinations at the *barre* each day that include *tendu*es it is possible to calculate how long it is before the *tendu* becomes automatic. *Tendu* exercises in the Academy Method will typically include 16 *tendu*es in each direction, noting that the exercise is repeated on each side. This being the case, with four directions (front, *à la seconde*, back and again *à la seconde*) then each time the exercise is done the dancer will do 64 to each side, or a total of 128. With two such exercises in each class, that makes a total of 256 per day. If a dancer takes 5 classes per week, that equals 1,280 per week. In this way, it will take approximately 80 weeks (or 20 months), roughly 2 years, for the action of a *tendu* to become automatic. Granted, beginning dancers do not take class that often, and at the early stages of training exercises are not that extensive.

ESTABLISHING MUSCLE MEMORY

In Level 1 training (expected to last 2 years), there is only one *tendu* exercise given in class normally, and the action is only repeated 8 times, but just *à la seconde*, and class is taken just three days per week. Therefore, by the end of the first two years of training, the dancer will have done about 2000 *tendu*es. At the next level, also approximately 2 years, the students do 8 *tendu*es but in all directions, and they have class four times per week. And so they will perform the *tendu* roughly 31,000 times in those years, bringing the total to 33,000, one third of the way there. In Level 3, class is taken 5 times per week, and now the second *tendu* exercise is added to class, but the repetition is still only 8 per direction. These two years the student will perform the *tendu* 51,000 times, bringing the total in their lifetime to 84,000. Therefore, when they arrive at Level 4 in the Lower School, where they now do the full 16 in each direction for two exercises and take class 6 days per week, (a total of about 1540 per week) they will accomplish the requisite 100,000 *tendu*es within 12 weeks. So midway through the first year of Level 4, the dancer's body is now performing *tendu* automatically. This is also true of *dégagé, grand battement, ronde de jambe* and other exercises.

When exercises are given without this type of repetition, muscle memory takes much longer to become part of the dancer's world, and they will be frustrated at their attempts to master steps.

To remove intensive focus on repetition from the method would result in half-learned, compromised, or misunderstood steps and sequences. The dancer, without this repetition, would also apply what was usual in their cumulative rather than truly embrace what is new, different and specific of what is being learned. What's more, they lose out on early development of muscle memory.

And so, repetition is a given in classical dance training. This being the case, as you have seen, there are predictable results, and preventable problems. To explore these potential problems, it must be understood what some of the challenges are.

The main challenge is that the muscles, or muscle groups, being repetitively used will get over-worked. This is, indeed, part of the design, and there is nothing wrong with it (see the next section "Exhaustion" in this chapter). Without this sort of repetition, putting the body into what is called an "anaerobic" state, the dancer will not develop the necessary body functions to be a high performing artist.

But the outcome of the early experiences with this type of maximal working of muscles, specifically cramps, is largely possible to avoid through the development of regular preventative hygiene and diet. The muscles that are over-worked will become depleted of sodium, calcium, potassium and magnesium. Together, these are called "electrolytes." The depletion of these electrolytes in the muscles will cause cramps anytime from during the training session to within the next 72 hours unless sodium, calcium, magnesium, and potassium are replenished. It is possible to avoid these cramps through diet and dietary supplements. A diet rich with these minerals is the very best preventative against muscle cramps.

The learning process does include cramps at times, and these will be a very good reminder to the dance student to take the supplements they have been told to take, and to develop much more rigorous stretching and cooling down routines.

EXHAUSTION

Applying the principles of movement as they relate to classical theatrical dancing allows the dancer to make intentional use of all elements of motion with absolute efficiency, to the maximum degree appropriate, in order to achieve artistic communication with the audience. Each of these goals is trained into each dancer. Yet absolute efficiency of movement is not something a dancer learns to do. It is achieved by the absence of effort; the allowance without obstacle of all relevant forces.

When the body is exhausted, utterly exhausted, yet is demanded to perform a movement, it will override the obstacles of mind, diminished energy supply and resistant circumstance. The body itself, independent of the dancer, will perform at absolute efficiency.

Therefore, exhaustion is carefully designed into training so as to achieve this goal. A dancer who is pushed into super hyper-aerobic exercise through repetition and careful sequencing of muscle uses and coordination will achieve absolute efficiency. And just to have gotten to this point also means that the movement becomes automatic, therefore is performed naturally as well.

PLACEMENT AND BALANCE

Placement in classical dancing refers to the relative unity of the entire body as it takes on each form demanded of it. Placement includes being balanced, but refers more to the overall line, and harmonious unity of the body's positions as it flows through the movements of a combination. In other words, while a *pirouette en attitude en dehors* must be balanced so that the dancer does not fall, the placement of the turn has to do with the entire body being correctly placed in the form of an *attitude* while executing the turn.

PROPER PLACEMENT

Normally, proper placement means the hips are level and square to the relative "front" of the position, the arms are correctly positioned, the head and shoulders are correct, the *pointe*d foot is aligned so that the second toe is in line with the center of the leg, the spine is lifted or flexed as required, etc. And then all of that must be in a balance.

ABILITY TO BALANCE

The body balances. This is a statement of absolute fact. Whatever food we eat, the body will balance the intake of that food such that if we eat high caloric foods the body will become fat, if we eat food we are allergic to the skin will become itchy, etc.

The fact that the body balances can be directly applied to dance, for when the body is put into a position, the body will automatically do everything to balance that position. When a person slips suddenly and unexpectedly, their arm fly out to the sides or up in the air. If you study slow motion video of people slipping, you will see that the arms, legs and head will all go in the direction needed to balance the sudden shift in position. Likewise, if a person slowly lifts one leg, the body will slowly adapt to that and move its parts into positions that counter balance the lifted leg.

BALANCE AND TURNS

So when we demand of our body to perform a *pirouette*, the question of balance should be moot; but it isn't. Why? Again, if you study slow-motion video of dance students attempting *pirouettes*, you will see that instead of going immediately into the position in which they will turn, they instead go gradually into a number of intermediary positions on the way to the turning position. If you study the video again, you will see that as each intermediary position occurs, the body begins to adjust to balance that position. The problem is that most dancers change position so many times on the way to the turning position that the body cannot balance the movement except by becoming either very tense, or just falling out of the turn.

SPEED OF ATTACK

As you teach your students about balance, have them do positions quickly rather than slowly. In academic *pirouettes,* the working leg performs a *grand battement passé* as the ball of the standing leg presses down. Both movements create the lift for the turn. Meanwhile, the head immediately turns around[4] and usually one arm will travel from 2nd position to either middle-5th position or to a *pirouette* position.

---

[4] Remember that the head leads the movement in every first turn in a sequence. Should there be a second turn or multiple turns, then spotting begins with the second turn.

These things all happening simultaneously, and very quickly, allows the body the simplicity of having only to balance a single position—that in which the dancer will turn—rather than having to counterbalance every intermediary position.

AUTOMATIC BALANCE

There are many exercises in the Academy Method that give the dancer practice going immediately into the final position. Very soon the dancers will be balancing automatically and will not have to fight for a balance, or timidly lift the hand off of the *barre* repeatedly "testing" their balance. Anyone who has ever danced on a stage, even if it is at amateur hour, knows that when you are dancing you do not have time to test your balance – either you balance or you don't. And so the quicker the dancer can get to the final position, the easier the job the body has to balance that position. And as the dance student repeatedly demands the body to balance instantly, the body will simply accept this as the norm. At this point balance becomes something automatic and unremarkable, giving the dancer that much more energy to focus on musicality, phrasing, dramatic presentation, and other interpretive elements of their performance.

LEVELS OF FOOT

There are five levels of the standing foot in classical dance. Below is the list of them and instances in which they are used.

Á TERRE

When a dancer stands on the sole of their foot, it is called *à terre*, meaning "on the earth". While this seems simple and as if there is nothing at all to learn about it, that is far from the case. When a dancer stands on their foot it is presumed they are in a dancing posture, and so the weight on their foot is centered at the center of the stance platform of the foot.

The stance platform of the foot is the entire area of contact with the ground upon which they stand. If a dancer is standing on one foot, then the stance platform is that foot and the dancer's weight should be centered at the point on the floor directly below the high point in the arch of that foot. A dancer should never be standing with weight centered on the heel of the foot, and rarely on the ball of the foot.

When a dancer is standing on two feet, the stance platform is the entire area beneath the dancer that is supported collectively by the joint footprint of both feet. Therefore, if a dancer is standing in 2nd position, the stance platform is all of the area from the outer most parts of the feet, and from the forward most part (the line between the big toes) to the rear-most part (the line between the heels). And the weight must be centered at the very middle point of this, which will be a spot between the high point of both arches.

NOTE: All points of contact between the feet and the ground on the stance platform should support precisely the same amount of weight. There should not be more weight on the balls of the feet, on some toes rather than others (often the little toes are not even on the ground because dancers have turned their feet out too much and thus rolled onto their arches).

QUARTER POINTE

In the quarter *pointe* positioning of the foot, the center line of the first metatarsal bone is at a 45° angle to the floor, with the weight centered on the ball of the foot just behind the second toe.

Quarter-pointe is used for the start of all *pirouettes* and in training exercises for pre-*pointe*[5] students.

DEMI-POINTE

In *demi-pointe* the central line of the first metatarsal bone is at a 90° angle to the floor. *Demi-pointe* is used for most dance movement, and is the position at the end of *pirouettes tire bouchantes*. With the metatarsal bone perpendicular to the floor, it is the highest a dancer can be on their foot, and is a position from which movement in any direction is possible. It is also a position in which the dancer still has control of their weight and can move that weight at will.

NOTE: Remember that the central line of the first metatarsal bone is from the center of the metatarsal joint to the center of the joint in the arch of the foot.

THREE-QUARTER POINTE

In three-quarter *pointe* the center line of the first metatarsal bone is at a 91 ° or greater angle to the floor. This position is only used in three instances in

---

[5] The use of muscles in the leg and hip in the *quarter-pointe* position in soft shoes is the same as the set and use of those muscles *sur les pointes* in toe shoes.

all of classical theatrical dancing: 1) when a movement ends with the dancer lifted up (mostly for men at the end of a male variation that might end in a locked, high-fifth position of the feet); 2) in a *piqué* that is a preparation in which the direction reverses; or 3) when doing turns such as *piqué jeté en tournant en dedans*.

This position is actually lower to the ground than on *demi-pointe* and is a locked position of the foot and hip. To be free of the position the dancer must bring the metatarsal bone back to a purely vertical line so they can regain control over their foot.

FULL POINTE

This is done only in *pointe* shoes. In *full-pointe* the set of the hip and use of leg and torso muscles is the same as *quarter-pointe*. There is an entire certification program for instructing dancing *sur les pointes*.

ELEVATION

Elevation on one or both feet is used in classical dance quite often. It is a way to get going, a way to turn on one foot, a way to balance. There are only four ways to elevate on the foot.

NOTE: Whenever the body is doing a movement in which it will be elevated, or leave the ground, the top of the head leads the way and the knee caps are the first to arrive. This is a law of movement.

LEVÉ

Levé ("to be elevated" is past tense of the French verb "lever" which means "to go up"). In ballet there are four ways this happens.

ÉLEVÉ

Élevé means "to rise" and in ballet is when the dancer presses downward with one or both balls of the feet so that the body will rise. In this movement, the center of balance of the body travels from the center of the arch of the standing foot (or feet) to the ball of the foot, or between the balls of the feet. In this movement the entire body changes position relative to the spot on the ground over which their weight had been previously centered.

RELEVÉ

Relevé means "to go up again" and is derived from the situation in which one is already on the ball of their foot and they will return to this position. To be on the ball(s) of ones foot presumes you are balanced there. To put your heel down and go up again indicates the need to have maintained the balance point, since you will be returning to it.

In a *relevé* the dancer maintains the same balance by springing up onto the ball (or *sur les pointes*) of the foot. The same balance point is maintained when the ball of the foot is brought under the center of the hip. In this movement, the body remains in the same point in relation to the ground below them, and instead of moving the body balance point to the ball of the foot, the dancer brings the ball of the foot under the center of the body.

This is done with a springing action in which the heels push the body away from the floor and in the brief instant that the body is airborne, the ball of the foot is quickly brought under the foot. The amount that the dancer "jumps" into the air is only enough to fit the length of the extended foot. Therefore, when a dancer springs up in a *relevé*, there is no landing bounce of the body on a straight leg.

EN LEVÉ

En levé is when a dancer's body is lifted by an outside force so that they end up balanced on the ball of an extended foot. This happens either in partnered passages, or when the dancer uses their arms on a stabile object so as to lift the body up.

PIQUÉ JETÉ

This movement is when the dancer's body weight is in the bottom of a *demi-plié* and they push off with the supporting foot using the action of a *frappé* to arrive on a fully straightened leg either in *demi-pointe*, *three-quarter pointe*, or *sur les pointes.* In a *piqué jeté* the moment the body arrives on the next foot the body is in its full position.

This means that the body is airborne between the legs, and just as with *relevé* there is no landing bounce. The body is propelled upward just the exact precise distance of the fully extended leg, so it is as if the body stops on a breath. And because the ending position is accomplished all at once in an instant, it will be balanced.

FINDING CENTER

The human body has bilateral symmetry, though no body is precisely symmetrical. The center line of the body is where the mirrored sides come together. In classical dance, one dances *from the center line*[6] of the body.

There are many steps in which the body is neither on one foot or the other, but is indeed between the legs. *Enchainement déboulé*[7] is one such movement, as are walking and running.

FIRST POSITION MOBILITY

When the body is standing in 1st position, the weight is between the legs. Smooth locomotion is achieved by having the body remain with its balance point in the center of the two legs, so that with each successive foot fall the body just continues to move smoothly forward (or backward). If the body comes to rest on each foot, it will have a swaying, side to side movement, most often associated with seduction or drunkenness. Likewise if the feet are brought into the center with each step, there is a waddling effect of the feet that is quite comical.

When walking or running, the body is actually falling past the leg it is on over and over again. When dancing, no matter how long a dancer may be cresting

---

[6] This phrase was changed in the 1950s by the late choreographer George Balanchine to be "dance on the center line." This change of a single word results in an entirely new aesthetic, which Mr. Balanchine himself intended to represent *Avant Garde* dance. By the late 20th century this style was mistaken for classical ballet.

[7] Known in the 20th and 21st centuries as "*Chaînée*" Turns.

on the top of one leg, the body is in an arc of motion that beyond the apex is falling toward the next leg.

CONTROLLED FALL

To dance, the dancer learns to control the fall so precisely that an ability is developed to perform endless permutations of movement, decided by choreographers, that include turns, jumps, sliding motion and much more. It all blends together in a form of movement so expressive that it is one of the highest art forms that exists.

It is this controlled falling that is studied in classical theatrical dance classes. The Academy Method is based on the fundamental principles of movement as apply to classical theatrical dancing.

BALANCE TOWARD WORKING SIDE

To control the fall, a dancer must be able to go in any direction at any moment. Therefore, the dancer must be on the very top of their leg, for only at the very apex does there exist the possibility of movement in any of the 360° range of potential direction.

When a dancer is standing in 1ˢᵗ position, both legs are at this maximum height. And when a leg is removed, to remain there takes a great deal of strength. The muscle that holds the hips level when on one leg is called the *gluteus medias* and it goes from the *greater trochanter* to the flange of the pelvic bone that forms the hip. The other muscles involved in this miraculous ability of dancers are the *iliotibial* band (which connects to the outside of the knee on the bottom and above the *gluteus medias* connecting to the same bone of the hip. These two muscles hold the pelvis, and subsequently the working side of the body, erect in 1st position balance even when only one leg is on the ground.

The other muscle in this intricate web of miracle producing anatomy is the *psoas*. This muscle attaches to the *femur* bone on the inside of the leg near and just below the groin, and then travels up through the opening in the center of the pelvis to connect to the front of the spine just behind the lungs. The *psoas*[8] holds the spine erect and lifts the abdomen up so that we don't have a pot belly.

All of these muscles make it possible for a dancer to achieve a balance without sitting on the hip of the supporting leg, without tilting the supporting leg into the diagonal of each leg is in 5th position. Dancers must always balance toward the working leg, which activates these muscles and establishes a level pelvic basin, and freedom use the legs and turnout to the maximum advantage.

---

[8] Another amazing fete possible, in part because of the *psoas*, is that when the trained dancer stands on one or two legs, and the *erector spinae* muscles (on either side of the spine) work together, the dancer is able to lift the front of the pelvic girdle up so that the pelvis isn't resting on the *femur* bone. This is how a dancer can spring down from full pointe, and many other things.

STRUCTURING A BARRE

When putting together a class it is important to know who the students are and what they have studied. Most likely you will know them well, and have worked with them often. If you are teaching the Academy Method, then it is likely you are teaching in a school with serious students who aim to become professional dancers one day.

SEQUENCE

The basic sequence of every *barre* is the same, in that it is a collection of exercises in a fairly standard sequence, yet there are some circumstances that will make a profound difference. The primary difference will be the developmental process of the dancers. In this introductory course, you are being exposed to the fundamentals and basic principles of teaching classical dance. And it is assumed you will be teaching students that are in the Lower School part of their training, and within that the students in Levels 1 and 2, who are just beginning to develop their muscles.

BARRE STRUCTURES AND STAGES OF DEVELOPMENT

With an eye toward examinations, it is important that the students learn the material they will be tested on. But more important than any test, production, audition or special occasion, is the physical development of the children, for that development will carry them forward in life.

The basic structures for *barre* exercises at that level are few. The class will either build strength, coordination, flexibility, or balance. These four elements are the primary categories for the development of young dancers.

PRIMARY CATEGORIES

Here are the factors to consider for each of these four:

Strength – development of secondary muscles most needed in ballet work;

Coordination – exercises that combine upper and lower body functions in ways that are essential to do the exercises;

Flexibility – flexibility is certainly a product of stretching, but stretch is useless unless the dancer is relaxed, so the exercises need to require of the body to relax; and

Balance – the most important thing to develop in order to balance is quickness and confidence, as well as trust in the body.

In the exercises below, pick out the ones that would best accentuate the element of development upon which you would build a class for each of these four.

We will take each of these and consider what might be needed to create a well structured class.

STRENGTH

In a class that has strength as its unifying underlying goal, one thing that will best support that is to have simple exercises with lots of re*petit*ion.

REPETITION

To build a strong dancer, they must be very well toned and have a good solid workout. Repeating a movement over and over makes it become automatic over time, but within a class the repeated movement begins to reveal itself. As the dancer adapts to the rhythm of re*petit*ion of a step, there is suddenly a much different view of that step. Perhaps the arm movement suddenly seems to really change the ease with which a movement is accomplished if it is done at a precise time, or in a precise direction.

In one class the students were given 144 *cabriole*s to do on the diagonal of a very large studio. At first the students thought the teacher was joking, being that he was a jolly old man who loved playing practical jokes on dancers. But he wasn't joking.

The look in the dancers eyes showed how terrified they were, and each assumed their attempt would fail. But the music began and dancers started working their way across the room. The first few *cabriole*s were leaden, but soon the dancers started springing up with ease, and after about half way some of them began to use inventive arm movements to help with the movement. In the end, most of the dancers finished the exercise and were fine. And all were shocked. It seemed all were stronger than they thought.

But strength alone is not necessarily effective or even evident. In fact, one very small movement, if done with perfect timing and nothing to detract the body from applying itself fully, can have more power than three people all working together in a grand effort.

EFFICIENCY

Efficiency is a large part of strength. And efficiency comes from several factors, the first of which is timing. When force is applied at precisely the right time, it has far more impact. Partnering is a very good example of this principle.

When needing to lift a partner, even in a *presage*, one only has to dead press the full weight of the dancer if there is no rhythm applied, and the dancer being lifted doesn't help at all. But after just a few attempts, a male partner soon learns that an initial toss upward that allows for getting directly under the body makes it so you are never lifting more than about one third of the body weight.

Repetition and efficiency are but two elements that serve in a class that is about strength.

EXERCISE

Create a *barre* sequence that will build strength in a dancer, but feature exercises that employ repetition and efficiency to help build the strength, and make existing strength go further.

COORDINATION

There are many difficult coordination patterns in classical dance. There are patterns such as the Diamond Step and Full *Contretemps temps de flêsche* and others that are complex coordination.

But coordination is far more basic than the hyper-complex steps. In classical dance the sides of the body are almost always doing different things, and even when the movement is symmetrical the sides of the body are doing mirror image of each other.

HARMONY

The first step in finding better coordination is to find the harmony that exists between diverse things. This harmony eventually comes from the dancer experiencing the body and its movements as a single organism, and the step as a single thing.

To experience the movement as a single thing, each element doing its part in the whole is to find coordination in the movement. Many steps, when slowed down, become awkward, and seem to do nothing more than tie the dancer's body into knots.

But when it comes together there is a coordination because of the way the parts play off of each other.

FOCUS

Often the element that brings the harmony is the focus or ultimate goal of a step. But like being on the field during a football game, it is sometimes very hard to keep focused on the objective.

And here the teacher can help a great deal, for every element in class is part of the structure, even what comments the teacher makes, to whom, when and in what tone of voice. Do not count yourself out, and remember that the students view you as the teacher, no matter how you view yourself. They assume you know, and that you can see everything. An encouraging word from you will go a long way with students.

SEQUENCE

Sometimes the problem is not a lack of coordination, but a faulty memory, or even a step explained in an incomplete way. Break things down into parts if you need to. There are some steps, like skipping, that become a disaster if the dance student is trying to do all of the steps in the correct order but they leave something out.

Slow down and examine what the student is doing. Ask them to explain the step to you, or to teach it to another student. Sometimes trying to explain it to another person will lead to a better understanding, and sometimes it will expose part of the sequence that has been omitted in the memory of the student.

EXERCISE

Build a plan for the *barre* in a class that will be about coordination. Make note of all elements you plan to use in order to get your point across and end up with dancers having a better sense of coordination.

FLEXIBILITY

Flexibility is essential for a classical dancer, both physically and mentally. Most times when a dancer is not flexible in one joint or area of the body, it isn't due to a physical problem, but the tension is coming from the mind. In instances like these it can be helpful for the dancer to close their eyes, with the music playing, and imagine their own body doing the exercise without any difficulty with flexibility.

RELAXATION

The most important element for a dancer to have in becoming more flexible is the ability to relax. Finding an exercise in which the body, or part of it, is completely relaxed can tip the scales and free the dancer from some sort of tension.

RELIABLE STRUCTURE

Often problems with flexibility stem from a lack of structural support, rather than a limit in the physical capacity of the dancer. When a dancer tries to do a step, but finds that the supporting part of the body simply is not available with the type or amount of support it needs, the movement is stilted and the dancer holds back. It is like having a slick spot on the floor, but being unsure of where it is. In such a situation the dancer is not going to approach the movement with the kind of abandon necessary to be truly flexible.

Find exercises, or create a version of one, in which one side of the body provides solid structure and the other is completely free and watch how much more flexible the dancer suddenly becomes.

STRETCH

Of course the most logical plan of attack in a class that builds flexibility is the element of stretch. But think outside of the box here. There are all kinds of stretch exercises, and a wide variety of ways to introduce the element of stretch that might be disguised.

Whenever a force outside of the body, or body part, that enhances or causes a stretch to happen this is called a passive stretch. Think through all of the steps at the *barre* and find the ones in which the dancer is having to rely on passive stretch to do the movement.

Be careful in a class focused on flexibility that the dancers remain within the aesthetic of classical dance. If there is a line that is exaggerated, however, point it out so that the students do not become confused as to what is an allowable range or placement in classical dance.

EXERCISE

Create a plan for a *barre* that focuses on flexibility as its main goal. And be creative here both with exercises and applications of principles of movement.

BALANCE

Balance in dance is essential. But for dancers it is necessary to balance in the 'real time' of actually dancing, not in some protracted moment of time beyond the structure of music, to test one's balance.

KINETIC BALANCE

In some steps it is the movement itself that creates the balance, rather than the position. Any turn that involves a *renversé* is relying on kinetic balance rather than structural balance.

ESTABLISHING BOUNDARY, KNOWING LIMITS

Remember Jenny Penney, the Royal Ballet dancer who was famed for her portrayal in the Bluebird *Pas de Deux* from Sleeping Beauty She finished her variation with extremely fast *enchainement déboulé* that ended in a *penché arabesque sur les pointes* with a perfect 6 O'clock *penché*. And there she balanced as the audience went wild.

She often took men's class, and in that class she always had trouble standing on a flat foot in her *arabesque*, falling in every direction. When asked what was wrong, since she had such perfect balance on stage, by a young dancer who *pointe*d out the discrepancy.

"Why do they cheer?" she asked.

"Because you balance on *pointe*!"

"No," she said, "it's because I balance on point right on the edge! And every day I need to find that edge so I can dance right up to it."

SPEED OF ATTACK

As has already been discussed, the body by its nature balances. And if the dancer gives the body a clear, quick position to balance, the body will balance that position. It is when a dancer is insecure, or unsure in their placement, and so gradually climbs to the final position then the body is being asked to balance a great parade of positions.

When a dancer takes the full position right away, the body will soon learn that this dancer means business and when they go into a position that is to balance or turn they will not back down, then the body will be come adept at instantly balancing any and all movement the dancer makes.

EXERCISE

Create a plan for a full *barre* that is to teach the dancers balance. Be sure that you are teaching real time balance in the context of actually dancing and nothing else.

BARRE EXERCISE GLOSSARY

GRAND PLIÉ

PURPOSE

1) TO STRETCH THE ACHILLES TENDON;

2) TO ESTABLISH CONTROL OVER BODY

DEMI PLIÉ

PURPOSE

1) LANDING FROM JUMPS,

2) JUMPING INTO THE AIR

PARTS

1) bend knees

2) press heels down

3) straighten knees

4) lift up

BATTEMENT CLOCHE

PURPOSE

1) FREE THE HIP

2) MOVE LEG AS SINGLE UNIT

GRAND BATTEMENT

PURPOSE

LIFT PELVIS UPWARD

DEFINITION

Largest movement of the leg possible without moving any other part of the body

TIMING

Is done on upbeat of the music.

TWO-COUNT GRAND BATTEMENT

PURPOSE

1) LIFT PELVIS INTO AIR

2) EMBELLISH THE CREST OF ARC

TENDU

PURPOSE

ASSURE FOOT IS POINTED WHEN LEAVING GROUND IN JUMPS

REBOUNDED TENDU

PURPOSE

TO ACTIVATE POINT OF FOOT IMMEDIATELY UPON LANDING IN CONSECUTIVE JUMPS

TWO-COUNT TENDU

PURPOSE

TO MAKE SURE THE POINTING OF THE FOOT COMES FROM A HEEL SOLIDLY ON THE GROUND

PARTS

1) push toe down, leg to 2nd;

2) stretch to tip of the toe;

3) drop the heel to closed position; and

4) press the heel down.

DEMI-PLIÉ TENDU

PURPOSE

TO CREATE CORRECT BEGINNING FOR *JETÉ SAUTÉ* AND *ASSEMBLÉ*

DÉGAGÉ

PURPOSE

TO UN-POINT THE FOOT QUICKLY WHEN LANDING FROM JUMPS

RONDE DE JAMBE

PURPOSE

TURNING MOTION AND IMPETUS

IMPETUS

en dehors - forward movement of the upper chest
en dedans forward rotation of the heel

RONDE DE JAMBE EN L'AIR

PURPOSE

TO CREATE CIRCULAR MOMENTUM THAT CAN BE EASILY TRANSFERRED

GRAND RONDE DE JAMBE

PURPOSE

TO COUNTERBALANCE THE FULLEST CIRCULAR MOVEMENT OF THE LEG WITH THE TORSO

ADAGIO

PURPOSE

1) TO PREPARE FOR *PETIT ALLEGRO* MOVEMENTS

2) COORDINATION OF INDIVIDUAL STEPS

3) LEARN NEW STEPS ACCURATELY

ADAGIO EXERCISES

DÉVLOPÉ

ENVLOPÉ

ROTATION

FOUETTE

FONDUE

GRAND RONDE DE JAMBE

PENCHÉ

FRAPPÉ

PURPOSE

**PUSHING DIRECTLY DOWNWARD TO CAUSE
PROPULSION OR THRUST, AND LIFT**

ALLEGRETTO

PURPOSE

1) CENTER THE BODY

2) USE THE BODY WORK AS A SINGLE ORGANISM

3) SEPARATE FROM THE BARRE

ALLEGRETTO EXERCISES

PETITS BATTEMENTS

BATTUES SERRÉES

GAGLIARDE

ALLEGRO PIROUETTE

SOUSOUS

PAS DE CHEVAL EN TOURNANT

www.ingramcontent.com/pod-product-compliance
Lightning Source LLC
Chambersburg PA
CBHW061518180526
45171CB00001B/235